Dear Parent:
Your child's love of reading starts here!

Every child learns to read in a different way and at his or her own speed. Some go back and forth between reading levels and read favorite books again and again. Others read through each level in order. You can help your young reader improve and become more confident by encouraging his or her own interests and abilities. From books your child reads with you to the first books he or she reads alone, there are I Can Read Books for every stage of reading:

SHARED READING
Basic language, word repetition, and whimsical illustrations, ideal for sharing with your emergent reader

BEGINNING READING
Short sentences, familiar words, and simple concepts for children eager to read on their own

READING WITH HELP
Engaging stories, longer sentences, and language play for developing readers

READING ALONE
Complex plots, challenging vocabulary, and high-interest topics for the independent reader

ADVANCED READING
Short paragraphs, chapters, and exciting themes for the perfect bridge to chapter books

I Can Read Books have introduced children to the joy of reading since 1957. Featuring award-winning authors and illustrators and a fabulous cast of beloved characters, I Can Read Books set the standard for beginning readers.

A lifetime of discovery begins with the magical words **"I Can Read!"**

Visit www.icanread.com for information
on enriching your child's reading experience.

For Nola Peterson,
the best reading buddy on the planet
—J.O'C.

For my friend, reading specialist Michelle Carr,
who has given the gift of reading to a
generation of Pegasus students
—R.P.G.

For LGE, my Blue Fairy of the Books.
TY for the 3rd Act
—T.E.

I Can Read Book® is a trademark of HarperCollins Publishers.

ISBN 978-0-06-237784-5 (trade bdg.) — ISBN 978-0-06-237783-8 (pbk.)

17 18 19 20 LSCC 10 9 8 ❖ First Edition

I Can Read!

BEGINNING READING 1

Fancy NANCY Best Reading Buddies

by Jane O'Connor

cover illustration by Robin Preiss Glasser

interior illustrations by Ted Enik

Ooh la la!

I am so fortunate.

That's fancy for lucky.

I have a reading buddy.

On Mondays we read together.

Violet is in fifth grade

and very mature.

That means she acts grown-up.

She wears cool clothes.

"I don't like to match," she says.

"I like to look original.

That means different."

Violet shows me her feet.

Even her shoes don't match!

That night

I try on lots of clothes.

"I don't like to match,"

I tell JoJo.

"I like to look original."

Then I try reading to JoJo.

But she wants to play instead.

She is not a good reading buddy.

Not like Violet.

Violet and I like
all the same books.
Isn't that fortunate?

Sometimes I read to Violet.

I sound out the hard words.

"You are a great reader,"

she tells me.

"*Merci*," I say.

"That's French for thanks!"

Later we go to the cafeteria.

We eat and chat.

Violet wants to be

a librarian someday.

Me too!

Today Violet reads a funny book
about a girl and her little sister.
The little sister gets into mischief.
Mischief is fancy for trouble.

"She is like my little sister!"

I say.

"Mine too," Violet says.

Violet shows me a picture

of her sister.

14

At home,

I take a picture of JoJo

from the album.

I want to show it to Violet

next Monday.

But next Monday

I wake up with a cold.

I have to miss school.

I do not get to see Violet.

It hurts my eyes to read.

So my dad reads to me.

He chats with me too.

My dad is very kind.

But I miss my reading buddy.

The Monday after that,

Violet's class has a trip.

So we can't read together.

She waves from the school bus.

"That's my reading buddy,"
I tell Lionel.

Lionel and I sit on a low bar
on the jungle gym.
The high bars make us dizzy.
"I miss my reading buddy.
I won't see her till next Monday."

Lionel shakes his head.
"There's no school Monday.
It's a holiday. Lucky us!"
But I don't think
that is fortunate at all.

Monday comes.

At breakfast my mom asks,

"Why do you look sad?"

I start to explain about missing
my reading buddy.
But then the phone rings.
My mom answers it.

A minute later

my mom says,

"Quick! Quick! Get dressed."

Before I can ask why,

she scoots me upstairs.

I am tying my shoes

when the doorbell rings.

"Nancy, go answer it,"

my mom calls to me.

I open the door and there is . . .

Violet!

"I miss reading together,"

Violet says.

"So my mom called your mom.

You're spending the day with us.

Guess where we are going first!"

We are going to the library,
of course.
We pick out lots of books
to take home.

I get a book

about a girl from Paris.

Violet finds another book

about the naughty little sister.

After that

we go for ice cream.

We sit in a booth in the back.

Violet and I split

a banana split.

Then I read my book to her.

She helps me with the hard words.

I am so fortunate.

I have the best reading buddy

in the world.

Fancy Nancy's Fancy Words

These are the fancy words in this book:

Fortunate—lucky

Mature—acting grown-up

Merci—French for thanks

Mischief—trouble

Original—different